YOU
Won't
Believe
YOUR
EYES!

Design by Brian Bean

Cover computer graphic by Catherine Jordan

Edited by Jane Lind

Typeset by Attic Typesetting Inc.

Annick Press gratefully acknowledges the support of The Canada
Council and the Ontario Arts Council

Canadian Cataloguing in Publication Data

Crystal, Nancy.
You won't believe your eyes

ISBN 1-55037-218-1

1. Eye – Juvenile literature. 2. Vision –
Experiments – Juvenile literature. 3. Scientific
recreations – Juvenile literature. I. Tytla, Milan.
II. Eldridge, Susan. III. Title.

QP475.7.C78 1992   j612.8′4   C91-095288-4

Distributed in Canada and the USA by:
Firefly Books Ltd.
250 Sparks Avenue
Willowdale, Ontario M2M 2S4
Canada

Printed and bound in Hong Kong

YOU Won't Believe YOUR EYES!

Written by Nancy Crystal and Milan Tytla

Illustrated by Susan Eldridge

ANNICK PRESS LTD.
TORONTO, CANADA

To all children, Jocelyn, Sabrina, and Krysten included

M.T.

To my family and friends, for being there and believing

N.C.

photo: Richard Milne

Milan Tytla received his PhD in 1982 in experimental psychology, specializing in vision. His major academic interest is in children's vision—specifically how it develops from being well below legal blindness in infancy to its full young adult capacity.

Milan has worked as a staff scientist in the Departments of Ophthalmology at The Hospital for Sick Children and at the Toronto General Hospital. He is especially interested in the visual abilities of children and adults with eye and brain difficulties because, "We quickly learn a great deal about normal vision by studying the abnormal." Milan also teaches courses in perception on a part-time basis at the University of Toronto.

He has been intrigued with the wonderful and often mysterious ways in which vision works since childhood.

Nancy Crystal is a teacher, editor, children's book author, television scriptwriter and a mother.

Several years ago she attended the University of Toronto to study psychology. The material covered in her course on perception was particularly fascinating, especially the experimental component of her studies. However, Nancy was never sure she would have an opportunity to use her new-found knowledge.

Some time later, however, a stroke of inspiration struck and Nancy contacted her former professor. Over the next year his course in perception was reworked into a children's book of experiments, demonstrations and "how-to" activities.

Table of Contents

This book is about vision: your eyes and how they work with your brain. The book is divided into seven parts filled with experiments, things to do and things to make.
If you want to find out a lot about how you see, you can read the whole book from beginning to end. If you are interested in only certain things, use the Table of Contents to pick out the parts you want. Have fun!

You won't believe your your EYES!

The eye is like a camera, but there's much more to seeing than just taking pictures. For example, did you catch the mistake in this title? And what about these:

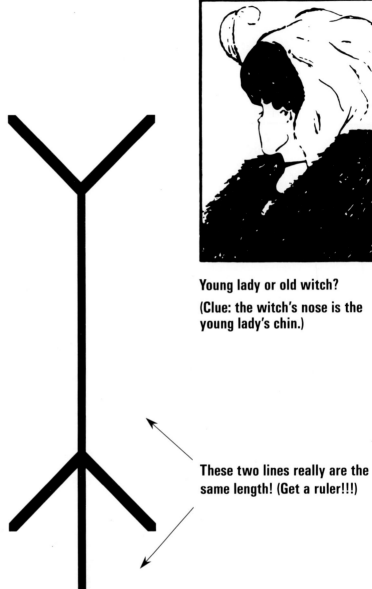

Young lady or old witch?
(Clue: the witch's nose is the young lady's chin.)

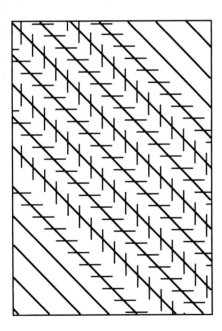

Which long lines are parallel? (All.)

These two lines really are the same length! (Get a ruler!!!)

Sorry, there's no triangle here. (See page 64.)

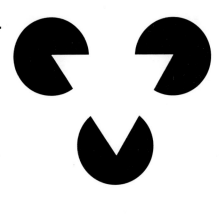

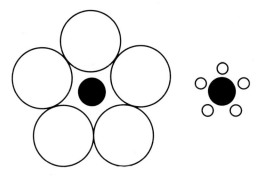

Are these black dots the same size? (Yes.)

That's right—the gray centre squares are identical!

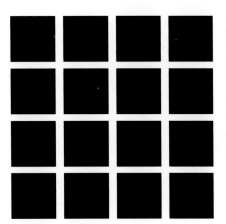

These types of illusion are fun, but they also tell scientists how your visual system works. So read on. Try the experiments and see for yourself. You'll be surprised—maybe even amazed. In fact . . . you won't believe your eyes!

Sometimes it's O.K. to see 'spots'. (Look for "ghost spots" at the intersections. See page 65.)

Better Than A Camera

What is round and leathery, full of jelly, wet all over and behaves like a video camera? Your eyes, of course. But no one has invented a camera yet that works as well as the eye. That is because no camera is attached to a human brain the way your eyes are.

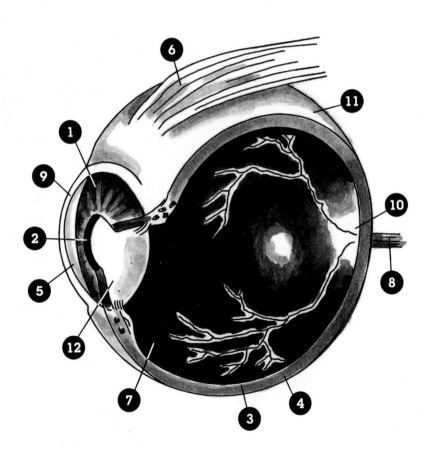

Your eyes are designed to let in light and send signals to your brain. Your brain makes sense of the signals your eyes send to it. In fact, vision only begins in your eyes. Your brain actually does the seeing.

If you could look inside your eyeball, this is what you would see:

❶ Iris

The circular muscle behind your cornea. When you say, "What beautiful blue eyes you have, my dear," you really mean, "What beautiful blue irises you have."

❷ Pupil

The black hole in the centre of your iris. It gets bigger or smaller to control the amount of light entering your eye. Look at your friend's pupils in a darkened room. What happens when you turn on the lights?

3 Retina

The lining at the back of the eye. It is as thick as a postage stamp and more delicate than wet tissue paper. 128 million special nerve cells change light into electrical messages that your brain understands.

4 Choroid

Between the sclera and the retina. In daytime creatures such as humans, the choroid is black to absorb light rays and prevent them from bouncing around. In nighttime creatures it is silvery to reflect as much light as possible. That is why cats' eyes glow in the dark.

5 Aqueous Humour

Means "watery liquid." It is behind your cornea, keeping it alive by bathing it with oxygen and nutrients.

6 Eye Muscles

There are three pairs for each eye. All six muscles work together to steer your eyes in all directions and to point them in the same direction.

7 Vitreous Humour

Means "glassy liquid." It is a clear jelly that fills your eyeball, like a water-filled balloon.

8 Optic Nerve

A cable containing over a million nerves that carry messages from your eye to your brain.

9 Cornea

The clear, transparent "window" made mostly of water. It focuses the light into the eye. Close your eyes, touch your eyelids and roll your eyes. That bump you feel is your cornea.

10 Optic Disc

This is the place where your blood vessels enter and leave your eye, and a million nerves lead to your brain. There is so much traffic here that there is no room for cells which receive light, and you are totally blind in this spot.

11 Sclera

The white of your eye. It is really a tough leathery skin that covers your entire eyeball except at the front where it becomes your cornea.

12 Lens

Right behind your iris is a clear, flexible lens. It changes its shape so things at different distances can be focused on your retina.

13

If you say to your friend, "I saw your dog in front of my house," you are really saying, "The light reflected from the dog entered my pupil and fell on my retina." This happens because your cornea bent the light rays and your lens changed its shape (thicker or thinner) to work with the cornea, making sure the image of the dog landed at the right place. If you are normal, your eyes had no problem getting the image of the dog in focus on your retina.

What If...

Have you ever used a magnifying glass in the sun to burn your name into a piece of wood? You were using the focal length of the lens to create a "mini sun" that burned the surface of the wood. You have lenses in your eyes, too. Can you imagine what would happen if you held your retina in place of the wood? Now you know why you should NEVER stare at the sun.

The distance from your lens to the image of the dog on your retina is called the focal length. In a normal eye, the focal length is about 17 millimetres, which is also the distance from the lens to the retina. In other words, they match. You can see how this works in the picture.

But what happens if the eyeball is too long or too short? If the focal length of your lens does not match the length of your eyeball exactly, you

normal

near-sighted

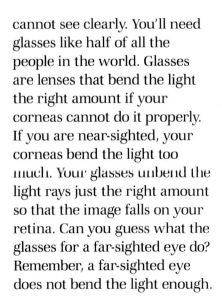

cannot see clearly. You'll need glasses like half of all the people in the world. Glasses are lenses that bend the light the right amount if your corneas cannot do it properly. If you are near-sighted, your corneas bend the light too much. Your glasses unbend the light rays just the right amount so that the image falls on your retina. Can you guess what the glasses for a far-sighted eye do? Remember, a far-sighted eye does not bend the light enough.

far-sighted

LET'S DO it!

Different lenses have different focal lengths. Usually, thick lenses have short focal lengths and thin lenses have long focal lengths. Find the focal length of a magnifying lens.

What You Need

magnifying glass
ruler

What To Do

1. Find a wall facing an outside window. (The darker the room the better.)

2. Hold your magnifying glass facing the wall.

3. Slowly move the lens toward or away from the wall until the scene outside is focused clearly on the wall. Make sure the scene is at least 6 metres away.

4. Now, measure the distance from your magnifying glass to the wall. That distance is the focal length of your lens.

5. Do the same thing with other lenses you can find.

Make Your Own Eyeball

Dazzle your friends with this enormous model of an eyeball that forms an image! It takes a while to put it together, but you can have fun making it and discovering how it works.

What You **Need**

magnifying glass (remove the handle and the frame)
ruler
round balloon
papier maché (strips of newspaper with flour-and-water paste)
waxed paper
paint (black, white and red)
masking tape
X-acto knife
1 sheet of construction paper or cardboard (cannot let light through)

What To **Do**

1 *This is the most important step.* Just like a real eye, the length of your model eyeball depends on the focal length of your magnifying lens. First find its focal length. (If you forgot how to do it, go to page 16.) Blow up your balloon to *EXACTLY* that length. An easy way to do this is to cut a circle out of cardboard. Make the diameter of the circle exactly the same as the focal length. Blow up your balloon to fill the circle exactly.

2 Cover your balloon with a heavy layer of papier mache. Let it dry overnight.

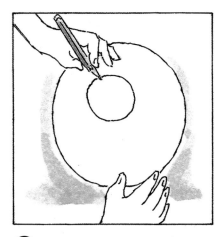

3 Trace the shape of your lens on one end of the balloon and ask an adult to cut a hole slightly smaller than your outline. Remove the balloon.

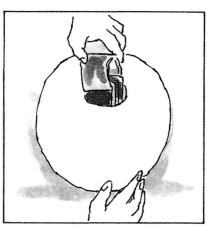

4 To make the choroid (see the diagram on page 12) pour some black paint into the eyeball and swish it around so that the inside is completely coated. Pour out the rest of the paint and let it dry.

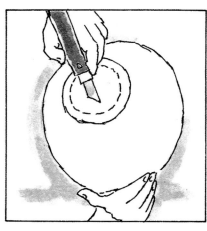

5 Trace the shape of your lens on the opposite side of the eyeball and cut out a hole slightly smaller than your outline.

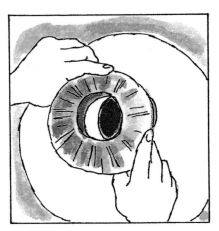

6 To make the iris, cut a circle, a bit larger than the lens, from your cardboard. Colour it blue, green or any colour. To make the pupil, cut a round hole in the centre of the iris about half the diameter of your lens. Tape the iris over the hole.

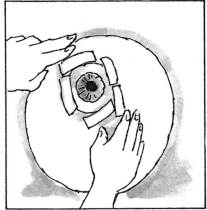

7 Tape the lens over the iris. You just attached the cornea.

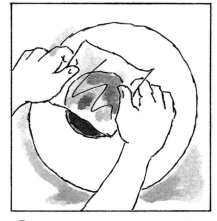

8 Carefully, tape a piece of waxed paper over the other hole in the eyeball. Make sure it lies flat. This is like the retina.

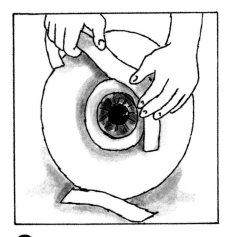

9 Cover the eyeball with another layer of papier mache. Slightly overlap the edges of the cornea and the retina to hold them in place.

10 When the eyeball is completely dry, smooth it with sandpaper and then paint the outside white. Be careful not to get paint on the cornea or the retina. For fun, you can add some ugly red veins. Let it dry.

Now you are ready to point the finished eyeball out a bright window. You should see an upside-down image on the retina. Explore the world with your new eyeball.

GUESS What?

Your friends can tell how bored or excited you are just by looking at your pupils. That's right! When you are bored, your pupils are quite small, but when you feel excited, they open up and become larger. Photographers have known this for a long time. Movie stars often have their photographs "touched up" with larger pupils because they think that makes them look more attractive. In fact, in the Middle Ages, women used eye drops called "bella donna" ("beautiful woman" in Italian) to dilate their pupils for exactly the same reason.

De-bugging the Bug-Eye Myth

You probably know that bugs have compound eyes covered with hundreds of tiny lenses. Most people think that this is how bugs see:

In fact, nobody knows how bugs see, but we can guarantee that this is not a bug's eye view. For bug vision to work in this way, a complete eye would have to be behind each lens. But, behind each lens is only *one* single receptor. The only thing any receptor can do is sense and signal to the brain how much light is present. One lone receptor *definitely cannot* send an image.

Bug eyes are really good at detecting motion all around the bug's body. That explains why it is so hard to sneak up on and swat a fly.

Frogs Use Their Eyes To Eat

Frogs have bug detectors built right into their eyes. When a bug flies in front of the frog, it knows exactly where the bug is and immediately flicks its tongue out to catch it. For its bug detectors to work, the bugs must be moving. In other words, frogs probably cannot see flies that sit perfectly still. A frog would die of starvation in a room full of delicious, nutritious, dead flies.

Even stranger is the fact that frogs use their eyes for more than just seeing. Watch a frog just after it has caught a fly. It is not blinking because it is choking on the fly. It is really using its eyes to swallow by pushing the fly, with its eyeball, down its throat.

HOW YOUR EYES WORK

When you open your eyes in the morning, they have three main jobs to do. They collect light rays; they form an image of what is in front of you, and they send messages to your brain.

The light rays bounce off whatever you look at—let's say

Picture This!

your chair—and enter your eyes through your pupils. The light first bends as it passes through your cornea and then through your lens, so the rays from the top of the chair land at the bottom of your retina and the rays from the bottom of your chair land at the top. This means that the chair is upside down on your retina. Your brain turns it right side up.

Your retina has two different types of cells: 120 million Rods and 8 million Cones. When the light rays land on the retina, the rods and cones change the rays into electrical signals that travel along your optic nerve to your brain, which uses these signals to tell you what you see. At the same time, you can decide whether to look at your chair or something else by using your eye muscles to move your eyes.

Here is an actual photo of a retina. If you could look inside the back of your eye this is what you would see. Your retina is a net made up of 128 million special nerve cells. Imagine that—128 million cells packed together in an area the size of a postage stamp!

Light ray strikes Rod

Rod   Cone

Signal sent to brain

The Blind Spot

What a busy place! So many blood vessels and nerves are going in and out there is no room here for a single rod or cone. That is why you are completely blind in this spot.

The Periphery

The rest of the retina is called the periphery (purr·i·fur·ee). It lets you see large, moving things out of the "corner of your eye" when you are looking straight ahead. It tells you *where* something is. The periphery contains mostly rods.

The Fovea

A tiny area on the retina where you have the sharpest vision. You use your fovea when you are looking right at something. Its job is to see *what* something is. The cones are the only kinds of cells at the centre of your fovea.

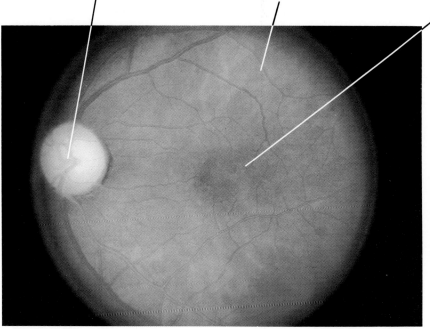

GUESS

What?

Your retina is the only place in your entire body where your doctor can see your blood vessels without cutting you open!

LET'S DO it!

The fovea and the periphery see very differently. Try these demonstrations with a friend and explore the differences.

What To Do

1 Have your friend sit on a chair and look straight ahead at something. No peeking to the side!

2 Raise some of the fingers of your hand. Starting from behind your friend's head, slowly bring your hand into view.

3 Have your friend call "stop" **AS SOON AS** she or he sees your hand. Ask how many fingers you raised. *(Chances are the answer will be wrong.)*

4 Keep moving your fingers forward until your friend can count them correctly.

5 Now switch places. See if you can do any better.

What did you discover? The "sharpness" of your vision improved as your hand approached your fovea. Your periphery could see only your hand.

There is another important difference between the fovea and the periphery. You need several objects of different colours for the next demonstration.

What To DO

1 Have your friend sit on a chair and look straight ahead.

2 Slowly bring one coloured object forward from behind your friend's head.

3 **AS SOON AS** your friend sees it, stop and ask what colour it is.

4 Continue bringing the object forward until your friend can tell you the correct colour.

5 Try it again, using things of different colours.

As you have discovered, the cones around the fovea see colour, rods don't. The periphery is colour blind.

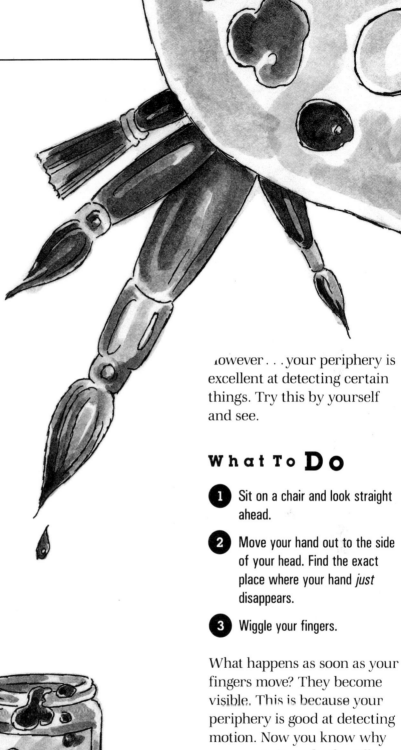

However . . . your periphery is excellent at detecting certain things. Try this by yourself and see.

What To DO

1 Sit on a chair and look straight ahead.

2 Move your hand out to the side of your head. Find the exact place where your hand *just* disappears.

3 Wiggle your fingers.

What happens as soon as your fingers move? They become visible. This is because your periphery is good at detecting motion. Now you know why you must sit perfectly still when you are trying to hide. Rabbits do exactly the same thing.

Why is it blurry when you open your eyes under water?

(*Hint: It has nothing to do with pollution.*)

Let's ask the same question a different way. Why does Jacques Cousteau wear a diving mask or goggles under water?

(*Hint: It is not because the salt water stings his eyes.*)

Remember, your cornea is made mostly of water. When light passes from air to water, it bends and forms an image or picture on your retina. When you open your eyes under water, light passes directly from the water to your cornea (which is also water). The light does not bend enough to form a sharp image on the retina and you cannot see. This is why Jacques Cousteau wears goggles—to keep air in front of his corneas.

HAVE YOU EVER

Wondered?

What about creatures like the Cormorant or the Nile crocodile, that look for food above *and* below water?

How do they do it? They have an extra, more powerful lens built into their eyelid, one that works when they close their eyes under water.

Testing Your Blind Spot

What happens at the optic disc—the part of your retina where there is no room for rods and cones? Does the world around you look like a photograph—with two holes in it, one for the blind spot in each eye? What a nuisance that would be!

Your blind spots are egg-shaped. The blind spot in your right eye is to the right of where you are looking, and you guessed it, the left one is to the left of where you are looking. So right now, why don't you see two huge egg-shaped holes to the right and to the left? The answer is easy with two eyes open. One eye can see what is in the other eye's blind spot. But even when you close one eye, there is still no hole out there. Let's figure out what is going on.

First, find your blind spot. Close your left eye and look only at the X with your right eye. Start with the page about 30 centimetres from your face and then slowly move it closer until the dot disappears. You have just placed the image of the dot on your blind spot. Now, turn the book upside down and try to find the blind spot in your left eye. Close

your right eye and look only at the X with your left eye. Slowly move the page away until the dot disappears.

Did you notice that the dot did not fall into a black hole but instead, just disappeared, leaving the page white? What do you think is happening here? In the same way, find your blind spot with the X and dot below.

What happened? Did the black line pass right through your blind spot? In other words, did you see something that was not really there? Your mind must have made a guess about what might be at your blind spot and then filled it in. BUT, it does not make *just any guess*, instead, it uses whatever pattern is right around your blind spot.

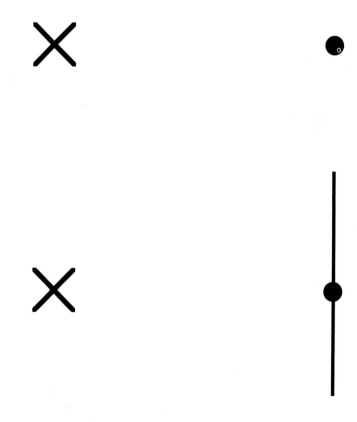

Try out the next three figures.

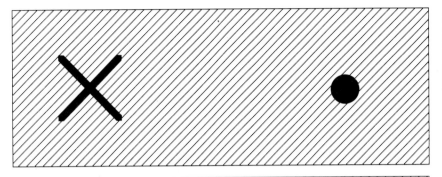

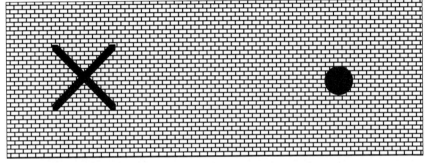

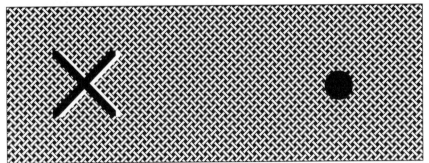

Your mind fills in to make up for your blindness in those spots, so you are not stuck with two black holes everywhere you look.

GUESS
What?

Chickens and roosters (and many other birds) go to sleep at sunset and don't awaken until sunrise. They have no choice! These birds have only cones in their retinas—no rods—and only rods see at night. After sunset, chickens and roosters are *totally blind*, and it would be very dangerous for them to stumble around blindly in the dark. So it seems that roosters really do have something to crow about at sunrise—*they can see again*!

Quick
AS A
Blink

It may surprise you to learn that blindness is a normal part of vision. You already know that you have a blind spot in each eye, and that you are temporarily blind when you first walk into a movie theatre. You are blind in other ways as well. By the time you reach this sentence, you may have blinked your eyes up to 20 times. Blink again. You were blind for about one third of a second. If you flashed the lights on and off in your room for the same length of time you would easily see the blackout.

actually jerk or jump. Convince yourself. Read on and place one of your fingers on the lid of one closed eye. Feel the jerks as you read. In fact, this kind of jerky eye movement is the fastest motion any part of your body can make. The amazing thing is that you make these movements all the time and you are blind for each one of them. Not just that, but you will make billions of them during your lifetime! Check it out for yourself.

Why do we not see a similar blackout during a blink? Since we blink up to about 20 times a minute, blackouts would be terribly annoying. It seems that your visual system cuts off the signal from the eye at the start of the blink and joins what you saw before with what you see after the blink. It completely ignores what happens *during* the blink.

A similar type of blindness happens even more often. As you read this sentence, your eyes do not slide smoothly from word to word. They

LET'S DO it!

Watch your friend's eyes jerk. Face each other closely and ask your friend to look back and forth quickly between your left eye and your right eye. You can easily see the jerky motion of the eyes. Now go to a mirror and do the same thing to yourself. You have no problem seeing that your eyes have changed position, but you definitely did not see the movement itself. Why? Was it too fast? No, you had no trouble seeing your friend's eyes move. What happened is that your visual system threw away any information before and during the jerk. Why does it do that? As your eye jerks from word to word, the old image lasts on your retina for a while. But because these eye movements are so fast, your system has to get rid of the last image to avoid overlap with the new one. Otherwise, words would just keep piling up after only a few movements and you would see this kind of jumbled heap:

Otherwise, words would just keep piling up after only a few movements and you would see this kind of jumbled heap:

We really need these split seconds of blindness to see normally. So, it seems that during your waking hours you actually do a lot less seeing than you think.

NUMBER
Crunching

You may have noticed this peculiar effect yourself. At times the bright, illuminated numbers and letters on the display of your microwave, VCR, stereo or CD player appear to jump or jiggle for a moment. If you have never noticed this, try staring at the numbers in complete darkness. If you get no effect, crunch on something hard, such as a carrot or melba toast. *They should be really jumping now*!

There are two reasons for this effect: (1) the numbers are actually flickering faster than we can see, and (2) your eyes are constantly jiggling in your head, and crunching on something hard produces an even larger jiggle. While you are holding your eyes as still as possible, those numbers are being "repainted" repeatedly on slightly different places on your retina. Every once in a while, and especially when you crunch, your eye does a big jump and a number is painted on a noticeably different place on your retina. Your mind does not know that your eye has moved so it assumes that the number has jumped.

Notice that while crunching, the numbers only jump up and down. That is because your jaw moves up and down and jiggles your eyes only in that direction. Tilt your head over one shoulder and crunch again. The numbers jump in the direction of your jaw motions, not up and down as before. You just proved to yourself that the numbers are not really jumping. It's all in your head!

31

Why Do We Have Two Eyes?

Can you think of any animals that have only one eye? Probably not. Most animals have one eye on each side of the head (rabbits, mice, beavers and horses, for example). These animals are plant-eaters *(herbivores)* and they are often hunted by meat-eaters

(carnivores). Herbivores have to be on the look-out for carnivores all the time. An eye on each side of a rabbit's head, for instance, allows it to see from the tip of its nose to the tip of its tail at any time. It can tell when an enemy is

huge overlap

left eye's view

right eye's view

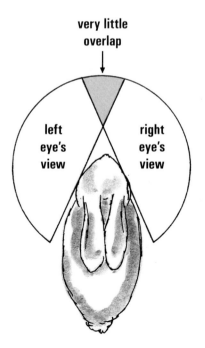

very little overlap

left eye's view

right eye's view

32

approaching because it can see almost completely around its entire body without turning its head. Animals with this kind of view have very little overlap in their two fields of vision.

But animals with eyes spaced apart and looking forward can see a large piece of the same view with both eyes at the same time. This two-eyed overlapping view, which is the same kind of sight we humans have, allows them to see depth in a very special way.

Some animals need to see the tiniest difference in depth for a variety of reasons. Perhaps they hunt well-camouflaged herbivores, or swing from vines and branches and have to know **exactly** where the next vine is. Others do close work with their hands such as picking fleas out of their fur or threading a needle. All these jobs require the best possible depth vision.

How do these creatures—and we humans—achieve such good vision? Each of our eyes sees a large part of the other eye's view. But each eye sees a slightly **different** view than the other eye. This difference is **VERY** important as you will soon discover. Your brain takes these different views, combines them and creates 3-D vision.

LET'S DO it!

Your pupils are between 5 to 7 centimetres apart. That means your left eye's view is slightly different from your right eye's.

What To Do

1 Hold your hand up in front of you with your thumb toward your nose.

2 Close one eye, then the other. Notice the two different views. Your left eye sees "around" the left side of your hand and your right eye sees "around" the right side of your hand.

3 Now open both eyes. With two eyes open, you have a single view of your hand, in depth. Seeing depth with two eyes is called *stereo vision*.

What is so special about stereo vision? Imagine that a speckled rabbit ran away from a pet store. Try to find it. Without camouflage, it would be easy to see.

What about a speckled rabbit that is completely hidden in the leaves and shadows? How can we see it? We have hidden the same rabbit in both of these boxes, but it is perfectly camouflaged. There are no clues to help you see it, but it *is* there!

Remember when you looked at your hand how each eye saw a slightly different view from the other? In these pictures, the one on the left is just what your left eye would see and the one on the right is just what your right eye would see. To see the camouflaged rabbit in depth, your mind has to combine the left and the right pictures. Right now, each eye can see **both** pictures. You can make a special gadget, a *stereoscope*, that shows the left picture only to the left eye and the right picture only to the right eye. When you find the rabbit, it will "pop" right out of the background, just like real stereo vision. It will look something like this.

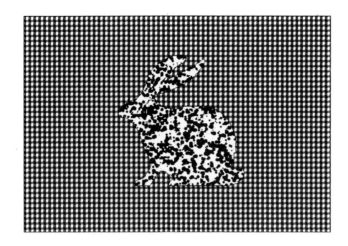

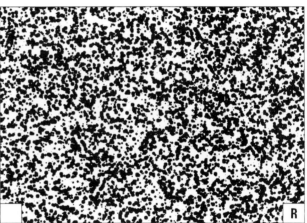

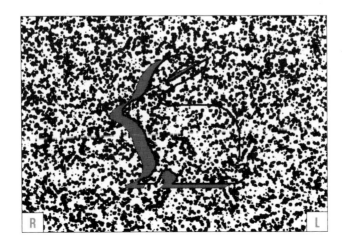

MAKE YOUR OWN
Stereoscope

A British scientist, Charles Wheatstone, invented a gadget like this around 1850. You need one of your own to see depth in all of our stereo pairs. You might want to ask a grown-up to help you. It takes a little adjusting to get it just right, but the end result is really worth it!

What You **Need**

a piece of wood about 40 cm long by 10 cm wide by 2.5 cm thick
2 pieces of heavy cardboard, 10 cm by 10 cm
2 identical rectangular pocket mirrors
pencil and ruler
plasticine
masking tape
2 bobby pins, hair clips or clothes pins
photocopies of diagrams and stereo pairs

What To **Do**

1 Measure the middle of your board along both edges and mark each with a dot. Draw a line connecting your 2 dots, as shown.

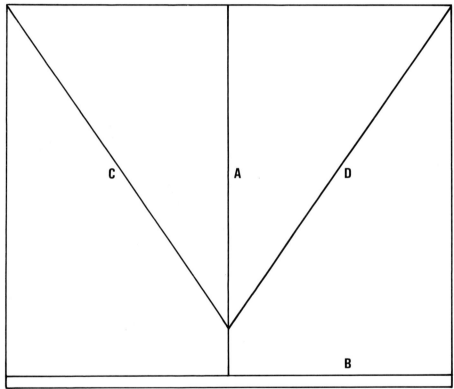

Diagram #1

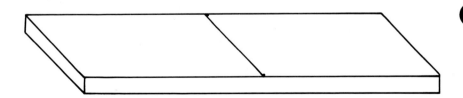

36

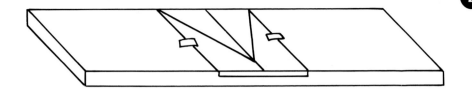

2 Cut out diagram #1 and line up line "A" of the diagram with the midline you drew on your board. Make sure the double line ("B") is along the front edge of your board. Tape it in place. Trace lines "A", "C" and "D" on your board using a pencil and ruler. Go over it a few times to leave a trace mark in the wood.

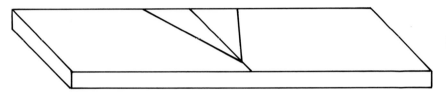

3 Remove the diagram and go over the trace marks on your board with a pencil and ruler.

4 Place a finger thick roll of plasticine along lines "C" and "D" on your board.

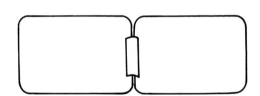

5 Lay your mirrors face down end-to-end, on a table and carefully tape the backs together along the touching edges. (Do not peel off the tape or it will ruin your mirrors. You can cut it later.)

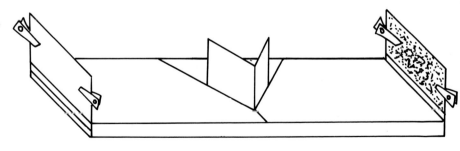

6 Bend the mirrors along the tape into a "V" shape and insert them in the plasticine. Line them up with lines "C" and "D". Gently tap them in place so that they sit evenly on the surface of the board. (It is important that your mirrors are right on the lines.)

7 Tape the cardboard squares on the ends of your board. Now you have a stereoscope!

8 Cut out the stereo pairs and clip them to the cardboard. (Read the labels and make sure the right and left diagrams are where they belong.)

9 Place your stereoscope lengthwise on the edge of a table or counter. With your nose touching the corner of the mirrors, look into the mirrors so that your right eye looks only into the right mirror and your left eye only looks into the left mirror. Adjust the stereo pairs so that both frames line up perfectly. You should see only one picture, not double. Stare at the picture and watch the rabbit "pop" out in 3-D.

10 For fun, switch the right and left stereo pairs to the opposite sides and see a rabbit-shaped hole instead!

(By the way, if you can't see the rabbit, even though your friends can, do not blame your stereoscope! About eight out of every 100 people are stereoblind. They do not have this kind of depth vision.)

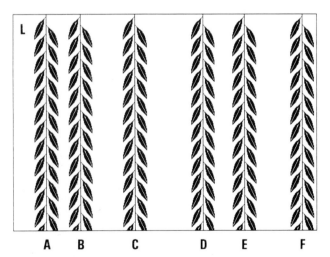

L

A B C D E F

Look at these stereo pairs with your stereoscope!

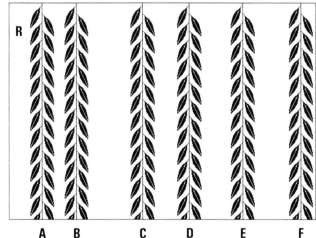

R

A B C D E F

O.K. Tarzan, which vine is closest—A, B, C, D, E or F? Look carefully. It's a long way down, if you miss!

GUESS

What?

Our ability to see depth is really amazing. We can actually tell if something is half a hair-width closer or farther away than its neighbour! It is so good, in fact, that it is one of the best ways to detect counterfeit money. If something on a counterfeit dollar bill is not printed in *exactly* the same place as on a real dollar bill, watch what happens when you view them together in a stereoscope. The first bill is real. What about the one under it? Is it real or is it "funny money"?

Stereoscopes are used by doctors to detect a serious eye disease, called glaucoma, which causes blindness if it is not treated in time. Remember the optic disc? (Look at page 13 again.) In a normal, healthy eye, the disc looks like a slight bump. In glaucoma, the disc has a dent in it. View these two discs in a stereoscope. If you were a doctor, would you start treatment for glaucoma, or not?

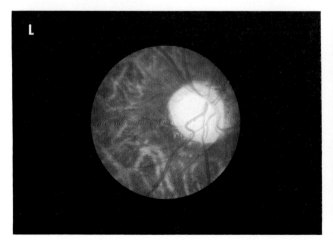
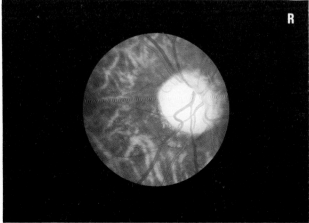

LET'S DO it!

Try this experiment to find out how two eyes are better than one for 3-D vision. You will need a friend to help you.

What You Need

a friend
bathroom tissue roll
pennies

What To Do

1 Flatten the paper roll as shown leaving a one centimetre opening.

2 Set the roll on a table between you and your friend. Stand about one metre away from the paper roll.

3 With only one eye open, give your friend directions (forward, backward, to the right, to the left) to position the penny over the opening of the paper roll and then drop it. Try it four or five times. Notice how poor your aim is?

4 Do the same thing with both eyes open this time. Notice how much better your aim—your depth vision—is with two eyes?

Eyes in Competition

So far, the stereo pairs have been very similar. Your brain had no trouble blending the two images into one picture. What would happen if the two views were totally different? Does the brain blend the two images into a combined picture?

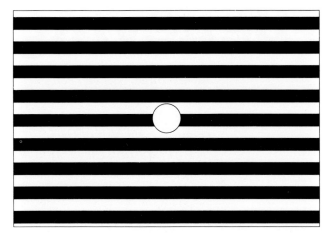
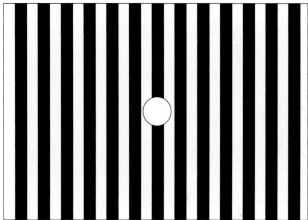

In this stereo pair, none of the lines match. Put them into the stereoscope and observe (this time left and right do not matter). Notice they do not bend into a checkerboard as you might have expected. Instead, the two images seem to be competing with each other, as if the brain cannot choose between them. Sometimes the whole picture switches. At other times only patches switch. But you will never see a checkerboard anywhere. Try another competing pair by putting a green card in one side and a red one on the other of your stereoscope. Also try a blue and yellow pair.

Even though it is true that your eyes work like a camera, there is much more to seeing than just taking a picture. What you see is affected by what you already know. Your brain is constantly using your knowledge to make sense of everything you see.

Seeing is Believing

For example, can you see the shape of a spotted Dalmation dog in all these spots? **(Hint:** *It is in the right half of the picture, sniffing the ground as it walks toward the upper left corner.)*

And what does this symbol mean?

B

It could mean many things. Let's add a little more information.

A

12   B   14

C

See, it can have two meanings.

I n the pictures below, do you think the children are normal size with a building in the distance or are they giants standing behind a doll house? Where the children are standing in relation to the building, that is, how they overlap, changes how you see their size.

These illustrations show that what you see depends on the surrounding information. Another name for this information is context.

A Swiss mineralogist, L.A. Necker, found this next illusion while he was looking at drawings of crystals. It is called a Necker Cube (it is about 150 years old). Stare at it for a few seconds. Did you see the cube flip? The shaded surface is sometimes seen as the back, and at other times as the front. If not, stare at it a little longer and the flipping will happen.

So, you can see the same thing in two very different ways. Since both choices are equally possible, there is no right or wrong answer. Your mind flips back and forth between the two equally likely choices. Scientists think that this shows how your mind works as it tries to make sense of what you see.

What happens when we add *just a little more* information? Here is the same cube with the same surface filled in, but now covering up some of the lines.

Now there is only one possible choice. Your brain has no trouble figuring out that the shaded surface is the one in front because it covers the lines behind it.

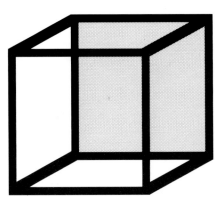

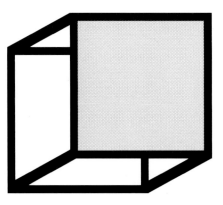

N ow we know that context (surrounding information) affects the way we see. What would happen if context did not exist? How would you make sense of the world you live in without any surrounding information? For example, when you see a car move, how do you really know it is moving? You know it is moving because your mind compares it to things nearby that are standing still. So what do you think would happen if you took away all context?

LET'S DO it!

Try this demonstration in a **completely** darkened room at night. It will not work as well in a closet because you know approximately how close the walls are. Remember, you do not want any context to give you clues!

What You Need

several friends
flashlight
small box with lid (big enough to hold flashlight)
masking tape
black construction paper or flat black paint (optional)

What To Do

1 Poke a small hole in the box with a sharp pencil.

2 Turn the flashlight on and place it in the box. Tape the lid on the box making absolutely sure *NO* light leaks. Use the black paper or paint to cover leaks.

3 Turn out all the lights, cover the windows and shut the door. The room must be completely dark.

4 Now, for a few minutes look at the tiny light coming through the hole. What happens? Sometimes the light appears to move and sometimes it stands still. Why? In a completely darkened room all context is gone. You have no visual clues because you cannot see your surroundings. Without any context, there is no way of knowing whether the light is moving. That is why sometimes it appears to move and sometimes it does not. What did your friends see?

The first people to report this strange movement were astronomers. After long periods of viewing through a telescope, they often saw stars jump around which they knew were perfectly still.

LET'S DO it!

Your brain judges how large something is according to how far away the object is. Let's do a simple experiment that shows how this works.

What To Do

1 Stare only at the white cross in the centre of the black circle for at least one minute. You are forming an *afterimage* of the circle on your retina. **This afterimage is always the same size on your retina.**

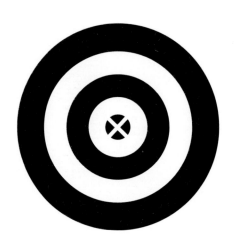

2 Look at your hand and judge how big the afterimage appears to be. If your afterimage starts to fade, blink a few times to bring it back.

3 Now, look at the wall farthest away from you. Did the circle just grow larger? Why does it look bigger when you know that the size of the afterimage has not changed on your retina? Your brain has just judged size according to distance. How large something is depends on how far away you think it is. This rule explains many illusions.

The picture on the left is just a flat drawing, but your brain sees it in 3-D just like the photograph on the right.

Which rectangle appears longer? The top one of course! Yet, if you measure them, they are exactly the same size on the page. (That means that they're also exactly the same size on your retina.) But, the top rectangle still looks longer. Just as you saw with your own afterimage, your mind thinks the top rectangle is farther away than the bottom rectangle so it appears to be bigger.

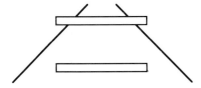

MAKE YOUR OWN
Ames Window

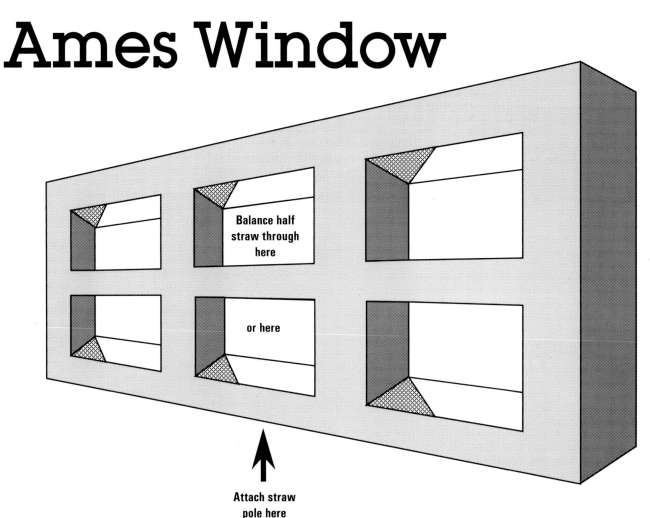

Balance half
straw through
here

or here

Attach straw
pole here

In the 1950s, Adelbert Ames, a lawyer turned scientist, was fascinated by depth cues. Here is one of his unusual demonstrations showing just how strong depth cues can be. This crazy illusion is so real that your friends might think it is a magic trick!

What You **Need**

construction paper
plasticine
paper clip
drinking straw (cut in half)
X-acto knife
record player
2 photocopies of this diagram

48

What To Do

1 Cut out the photocopies and trace one of the windows on construction paper. Cut out that window also.

2 Glue the three windows together with the construction paper in between the two photocopies. (Make sure the printed sides are on the outside.) Have a grown-up cut out the inner windows with an X-acto knife. Try not to bend the window while cutting.

3 Make two slits in the top of one of the straws and insert the window into the slits along the black line, as shown.

4 Stick the other end of the straw into a ball of plasticine. Place it in the exact centre of your turntable. Turn your record player on to the *slowest* speed and make sure that nothing wobbles.

5 Leave your record player on and step back between two and five metres. Keep your eye level with your window. Observe what happens. You know that your window is rotating in a full circle, but it looks as though it is flipping back and forth instead. Do you know why?

(HINT: Perspective and shadow are causing this effect. The large end of the window always appears closer to you whether it is moving or standing still.)

6 Now, using a paper clip, balance the other straw through the window as shown. Turn on your record player, step back and observe again. Doesn't it look as if the straw is passing right through the window? If it doesn't, give yourself more time or try looking at it with one eye only.

In this case, the illusion of the window's motion (flipping back and forth) appears to be just as real as the motion of the hanging straw. Since both motions are equally possible, you see the solid straw as passing through the solid window. The Ames Window is a great example showing how much of what you see happens in your mind.

Only
THE
Nose Knows!

All noses stick *out*. Of course!
What do you think would
happen if you saw a nose that
pointed *in* instead of out?

What You Need

plastic face mask
light opaque paint (metallic paint works
   best)
desk lamp (or any lamp without its
   shade)
sharp pencil
plasticine
record player

What To Do

1. Paint the outside of your mask with your opaque or metallic paint to be sure that no light can pass through the mask.

2. Stick the pointed end of the pencil into the bottom of the mask and hold it firmly in place with plasticine.

3. Place a ball of plasticine in the centre of the turntable of your record player and stick the other end of the pencil into it. Make sure it does not wobble when the record player is turned on.

4. In a dark room, shine your lamp at an angle onto the *inside* of the mask, as shown.

5. Turn your record player to the slowest speed and step back about two metres (6 feet). Watch the mask with one eye closed. Notice that the nose appears to stick out on both sides of the mask as it turns around! Try it again with both eyes open. If your mask has eye-holes, balance a straw through it in the same way you did for the Ames window. When rotating, the straw should appear to pass right through the mask!

Why does this illusion happen? Think about it. Real noses, noses that you've seen since you were a baby, point out. As far as your mind is concerned, this is the only way real faces can be seen in the real world. So, in spite of all other cues, you see that nose the only way you know how.

Nothing Really Moves At The Movies!

How do you know that something you think is moving actually is moving? Imagine these two scenes.

SCENE 1: You are staring at a tree when suddenly a dog races by.

This may seem like an odd question, but how do you know that the dog and not the tree is moving?

The answer is really quite simple. The image of the dog is sliding across one cell after another on your retina. Your brain assumes that if neighbouring cells are being excited in sequence, that thing is moving. The tree that you are staring at does not excite neighbouring cells in your retina so your brain assumes that the tree must be standing still.

52

SCENE 2: The same scene as before, but this time you do not stare at the tree.

Your eye follows the dog as it races by. If your eye is on the dog the entire time, its image is not sliding across your retina, but you still see the dog as moving. Obviously, there must be another way to see motion.

This time, your brain gets its information from your eye movements as your eye muscles turn your eyes to follow the dog.

Your ability to see the dog moving is not so surprising. However, seeing movement even when there is no real movement *is* surprising.

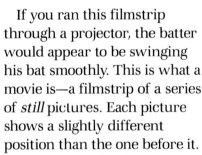

If you ran this filmstrip through a projector, the batter would appear to be swinging his bat smoothly. This is what a movie is—a filmstrip of a series of *still* pictures. Each picture shows a slightly different position than the one before it.

There is absolutely no real movement on any of the still pictures. A movie projector flashes one still picture after another onto a screen. Your brain blends each picture into the next one, giving you the *illusion* of movement. That is why we say nothing really moves at the movies.

53

GUESS What?

The idea of moving pictures all came about because of a $25,000 bet in 1872. California railway tycoon, Leland Stanford, bet that all four hooves of a trotting horse leave the ground for a split second.

(Stanford must have been pretty sure of himself—$25,000 in 1872 would be worth a fortune today!)

Stanford hired a photographer named Eadweard Muybridge to prove he was right. Muybridge set up several cameras at equal distances along the track to take pictures of the horses as they raced by. At the end of the race, he had several still pictures, each one taken just a few seconds apart

from the next one. The proof was in the pictures. Yes indeed, at certain times, all four hooves were off the ground!

In 1888, Thomas Edison worked with some of Muybridge's pictures and discovered how to get the illusion of motion from still pictures. He invented a large movie wheel, which held several still photos taken just seconds apart. When you looked through a little hole in the wheel while it was spinning, the objects in the photos appeared to be moving. This simple invention was the beginning of the giant movie industry.

54

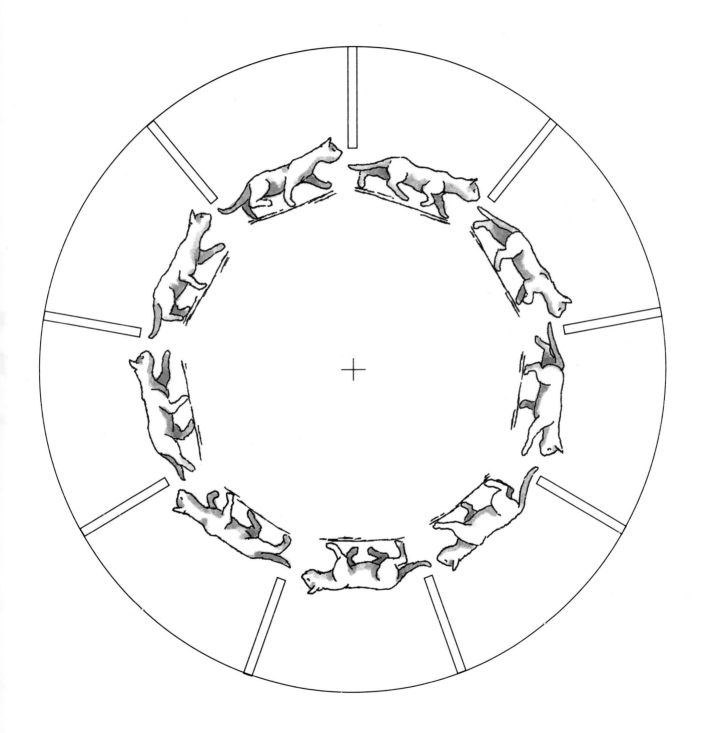

Make Your Own Movie Wheel

You can create the illusion of movement with this simple gadget.

What You Need

glue
photocopy of movie wheels
cardboard
X-acto knife
pencil
plasticine

What To Do

1. Glue the photocopied movie wheel onto the cardboard and cut it out around the outside edge.

2. Cut out rectangles around the outside edge (See the illustration). Cut a hole in the centre big enough for your pencil to fit through, so that the wheel can spin without wobbling.

3. Mount your wheel on the pencil with the printed side facing the point. Stick a ball of plasticine on the tip of the pencil to keep the wheel on.

4. Hold your wheel in front of a mirror with the printed side facing the mirror. Spin your wheel as you look through the little holes from the back.

More Motion Illusions

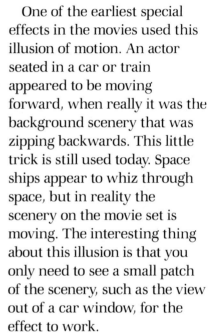

Movies are only one example of the illusion of movement. There are many others. Have you ever watched the moon on a cloudy, windy night? It looks as if it were sailing across the sky. Obviously, *the clouds* are moving. What is going on here? Your mind thinks that large objects are more likely to stay still while little objects can be moved more easily. Because the moon appears smaller than the clouds, your brain assumes the wrong thing is moving.

One of the earliest special effects in the movies used this illusion of motion. An actor seated in a car or train appeared to be moving forward, when really it was the background scenery that was zipping backwards. This little trick is still used today. Space ships appear to whiz through space, but in reality the scenery on the movie set is moving. The interesting thing about this illusion is that you only need to see a small patch of the scenery, such as the view out of a car window, for the effect to work.

You may have felt this illusion yourself. Remember the last time your car stopped next to a huge truck, waiting for the lights to change? As the truck moved forward, you probably felt as if your car was rolling backward. This illusion seems so real that the driver of the car often slams on the brakes—even though the car is standing perfectly still.

Another way to see motion that is not really happening is called *motion aftereffect.* You will have to shrink some heads to see it!

LET'S **DO** it!

Watch as the size of your friend's head changes for a moment or two.

What You Need

a friend with a good sense of humour
record player
photocopy of this spiral

What To Do

1. Read all the instructions before you begin.

2. Cut out the spiral and punch a small hole in the centre.

3. Place the spiral on the turntable of your record player and play it on the slowest speed. Your friend's face should be close to the spiral (about 30 centimetres).

4. Stare around the centre of the spiral for at least one full minute. (Have your friend time you or count to 100.)

5. When your time is up, *immediately* stare at your friend's nose. Your friend's head should appear to move away and shrink.

What would happen if the spiral spun the other way? Afterward would your friend have a swollen head?

How It Works

The vision center of your brain has special cells that detect motion. These cells are arranged in opposite pairs. For example, cells that send a signal for outward motion are paired with cells that send a signal for inward motion. As the spiral was turning on your record player, it appeared to be moving outward. After staring at it for a minute, your outward motion cells became too tired to send a signal. However, their opposite partner cells (inward motion) were not tired at all. So, when you looked at something that was not moving—like your friend's face—these inward motion cells took over and began to send *their* signal. That is why your friend's face appeared to shrink.

By the way, this process *must* be happening in your brain, not in your eyes, because your brain is the only place where these special cells are found.

GUESS What?

Our own motion can also help us see in 3-D. Have you ever noticed what happens when you move? The next time you take a car, train or bus ride, look out the side window and look at an object in the distance. Things in front of the object you are staring at move in a different direction from things behind that object.

Your visual system knows that when you are moving, things that appear to move in the opposite direction must be in front of what you are looking at. Things that appear to move in the same direction with you are behind what you are looking at. Scientists call this powerful cue to depth, motion parallax.

Most cartoons are filmed on a single sheet of plastic celluloid. In the 1930s, Disney Studios were among the first to use motion parallax in their cartoons to give them realistic depth. They invented a special camera that had many sheets of celluloid at different distances from the lens. Each sheet could be moved separately. With the camera focused on Snow White on a middle sheet, if they moved things in front of her to the right, and things behind her to the left you saw very real-looking depth and felt as if you were moving to the left. Snow White and Pinnocchio were the first cartoons to use parallax.

Many action video games get their illusion of depth this way, too. Next time you see such a video game, look for motion parallax.

LET'S DO it!

Finally, let's see how an object's own motion gives it the appearance of depth. Sometimes things are seen in 3-D *only* when they are moving. They look entirely different when they are standing still.

Try this experiment with a friend to see how you can get the illusion of depth from motion.

What You Need

bright lamp
long pipe cleaner or stiff bendable wire
big ball of plasticine

What To Do

1 Bend the pipe cleaner into a squiggly shape and stick one end into the plasticine ball as shown. Place the squiggle on a table top about 1 metre from a light wall.

2 Use your desk lamp to cast a shadow of the squiggle onto the wall. Place yourself where you can see the shadow but not the wire—stand beside the wire, for example. The shadow looks like nothing more than a flat, squiggly line.

3 Have your friend rotate the ball of plasticine slowly.

Suddenly, that flat looking squiggle "pops" into a 3-D shape! This effect of depth comes strictly from motion.

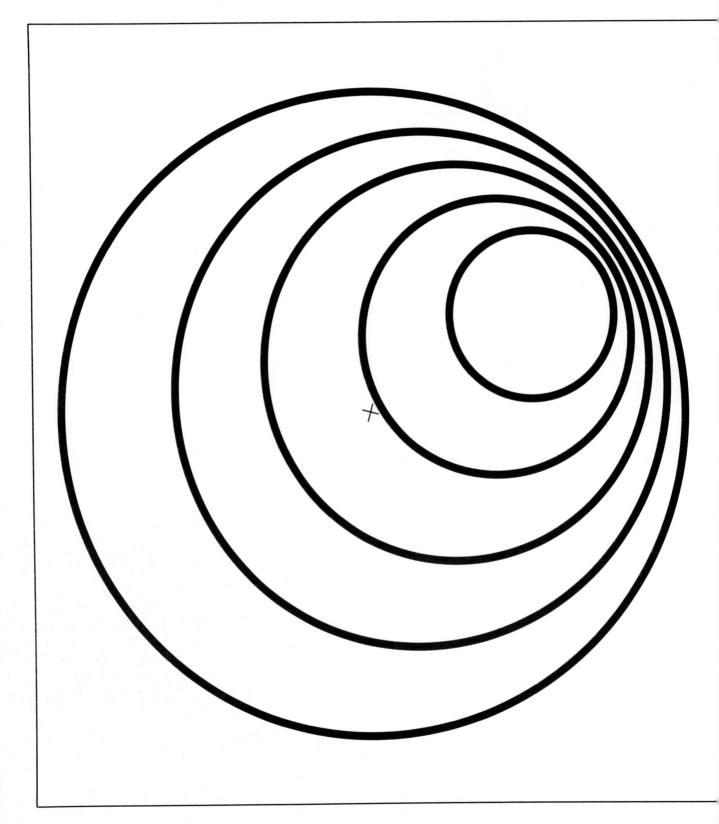

LET'S DO it Again !

Here's a different way that motion can make something look 3-D.

Photocopy or trace this diagram.

Place it on the turntable of your record player and let it slowly spin.

Doesn't it look like a cone in depth?
This illusion, like the others, comes strictly from motion.

Whiter Than White

Every object you see either gives off light (like the sun or a light bulb) or reflects light (like the moon or this page). When you turn up the lights in your room, objects become brighter. That is not surprising, but objects can also appear brighter for reasons other than the amount of light available. If you have two objects with the same amount of light, one can appear darker or brighter depending on how much light is coming from the space around it. Dark backgrounds make light things look even brighter and light backgrounds make dark things look even darker. Sound confusing? Look at these three examples.

What do you see here? Three Pac Men having a conversation or a triangle lying on top of three black dots? Doesn't the triangle look brighter than the rest of the page? Could it really be whiter than white? (By the way, the triangle is not really there. Cover the black dots and see for yourself.)

If you had a cardboard triangle lying on top of three black circles, the triangle would be closer to you. Things that are closer to you usually appear brighter than things that are farther away.

This diagram is called a Hermann grid. Think of it as a city map. The black squares are city blocks, the white lines are streets, and where the streets cross are the intersections. Do you see ghost spots at the intersections? The spots are not really on the page.

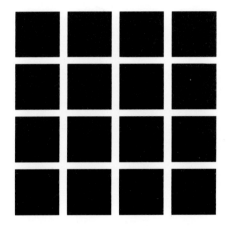

The amount of light that is reflected off the streets and the intersections is exactly the same, but you do not see the streets and the intersections as being equally bright. The intersections have a blurry spot that appears to be darker than the streets. Look at the grid again. There is more dark background around the streets than there is around the openings at the intersections. *Remember, dark backgrounds make light things look even brighter.* So, if the streets look brighter than they really are, the intersections will look darker than they really are by comparison.

If you still do not believe that the background is causing this effect, take away the background and see what happens. Cover everything except one street with two pieces of plain white paper. Do not let any black show.

Notice that the spots are no longer there. The street and the intersections are the same brightness. Are you convinced now that brightness depends on background?

Here is another Hermann grid in reverse. Do you see light spots in the intersections?

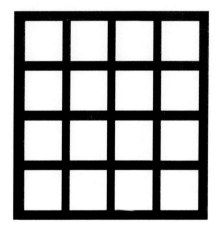

In this case, the streets are black and the squares are white. You know that background affects the brightness of the streets. Can you explain why the intersections appear lighter than the streets? (**Hint:** *light backgrounds make dark things look even darker.*)

LET'S DO it!

Look at these four squares.

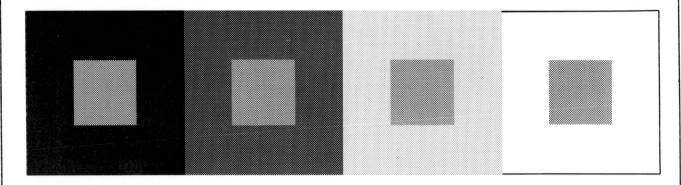

The four centre squares are all the same brightness. Convince yourself.

The amount of light coming from each of the grey centre squares is **_exactly_** the same, but we do not see them as being equally bright. The one on the white background looks darker than the one on the black background.

What You Need

a sheet of white paper
scissors
(a paper punch if you have one)

What To Do

Cut four holes out of a sheet of paper so that each hole is centred over each grey centre square. See—all the grey centres look the same.

All these examples have to do with contrast. Contrast is the difference in brightness between two areas. Your eyes can detect these differences because of the way the rods and cones in your retina are connected. There are 128 million of these cells but only about one million nerves leave the eye.

Only one million cables in the optic nerve carrying signals to the brain.

About 130 million rods and cones in the retina.

In other words, many cells combine what they see and send one signal to the brain along one nerve. If each cell had its own direct line to the brain, none of these effects would work. Direct lines would simply copy the image. It seems that the way each cell behaves depends on what its neighbour is doing, because they are connected. So, the cells that see the bright patch are affected by their neighbours that see the dark patch.

This is one way that your eye differs from a camera. The film in a camera does not show any of these effects—it just makes a copy of the picture you are taking. As you have seen, your eye does a lot more than just copy.

67

Figure THIS Out

Pretend you are making a TV commercial to advertise the super cleaning power of your new *Whiter Than White* laundry detergent. What backgrounds would you use for your socks and for Brand X's socks to make your socks look whiter and brighter?

Guess

Stars do not come out at night! Actually, they are out all the time. During the day, the sun lights up the sky so much that you cannot see the twinkling of a faraway star.

In other words, there is not enough contrast between the stars and sky. At night, stars appear because they now have great contrast against the dark sky.

What?

Background is not the only thing that affects brightness. What happens when you walk into a dark movie theatre on a bright, sunny day? It is hard to see at first, but after a few minutes, you begin to see the seats, the people and popcorn all around you. Something is changing. The lights in the theatre are not getting brighter. The rods and cones in your retina are getting used to the dark. The process of getting used to something is called *adaptation*. Your rods and cones are adapting to the dark. In this case, the brightness of things in the theatre depends on how much your retina has adapted. When you first walked in off the street, your retina was adapted to the light outside—it needed a lot of light to see. That is why everything inside the theatre appeared very dark. As you spend more time in the dark, your retina adapts to the darkness (it needs less light), so things slowly look brighter.

LET'S DO it!

Try this experiment. You will need either a bright lamp or a place outside in the sunlight.

What To Do

1 First, convince yourself that the rectangle below is the same brightness all over.

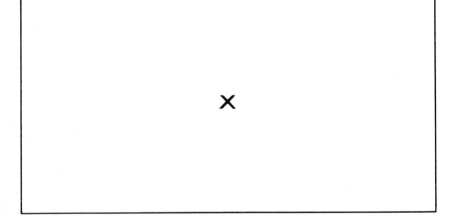

2 Now, cover half of the rectangle with a black card and stare only at the X—nowhere else—for at least one full minute. (The right side of your retina is becoming dark adapted while your left side is becoming light adapted.)

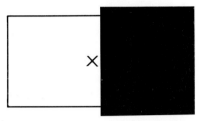

3 While still keeping your eyes on the X, quickly slide the black card away. Notice the difference in brightness between the left and right side? The right side, which was dark adapting now sees brighter. The left side, which was light adapting now sees darker. That is why it's hard to see when you first walk into a dark theatre.

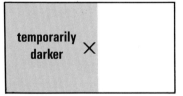

temporarily darker

4 Just for fun, make your whole retina return to normal. Watch as both sides become equally bright again.

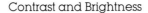

GUESS What?

We adapt to all kinds of things. Farmers are lucky that after being in the barn for a while, they do not notice the odours any more. But if someone walked into the barn wearing strong perfume, the farmer would smell it in an instant.

Why? All your senses are designed to notice *changes*. After a while, the farmer does not notice the barn odours, but the perfume is a new odour so he senses it right away.

Faster
Than A Speeding Streetlight!

Have you ever noticed that when the streetlights turn on, the lights at the intersections seem to come on just before the other streetlights? Also, if you happen to be looking down the street and the streetlights come on, it seems as if the lights are turning on in order, starting with the closest one first. Most of us think that is what is really happening. *They all come on at **exactly** the same time and the light from all lamps reaches your eye at **exactly** the same time!* The reason they *seem* to come on at different times, is because of a simple law: the dimmer the light, the longer it takes for the signal to reach the brain from the retina. Signals from the brightest lights reach the brain the earliest. That is why the lights that are closest to you appear to come on first. They are brighter than lights that are farther away and their image gets to the brain the quickest. Intersections are brighter because there are more lights concentrated in one area. Once again, the brighter the light, the faster the signal to the brain.

LIGHT AND COLOUR

Is Big Bird Really Yellow on TV?

What colour *is* Big Bird on TV? Let's find out. Find a patch that is white or yellow on your television set and look at it through your magnifying glass. Did you see any white or yellow dots? You probably saw only red, green and blue dots. How strange, but before we

can find out what is going on here, we need to understand light and how it works.

White light streaming from the sun is made up of tiny photons travelling in perfectly straight lines. Each photon shakes (vibrates) while it moves. Some photons vibrate slowly (we see these as red) and some photons vibrate quickly (we see these as blue). The other colours fall somewhere in between. Every photon follows a long wavy path. The distance from the peak of one wave to the peak of the next wave is called one wavelength. "Blue" photons are very energetic and have short wavelengths. "Red" photons are less energetic and have long wavelengths. Keep in mind, though, that even the longest wavelength is actually extremely tiny—about 10 thousand times smaller than the smallest grain of sand.

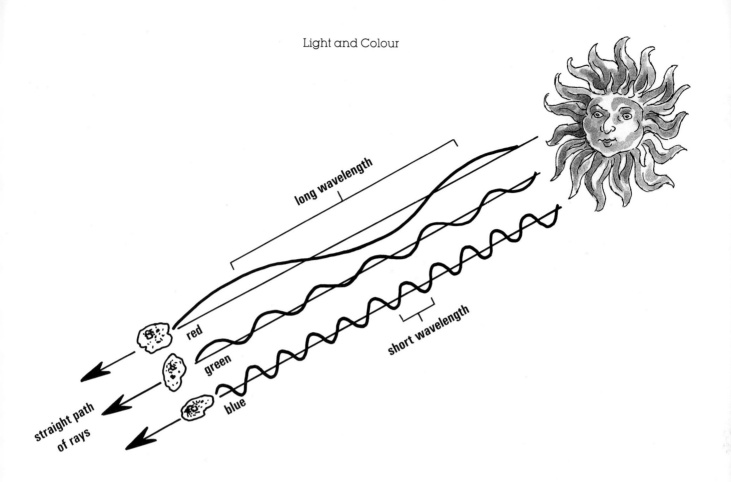

long wavelength

short wavelength

red

green

blue

straight path
of rays

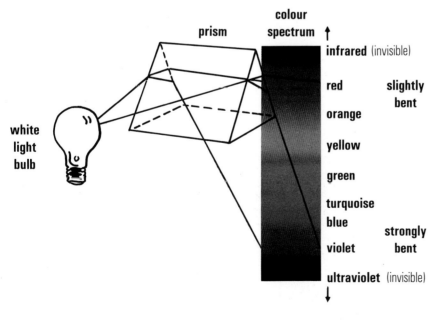

white
light
bulb

prism

colour
spectrum ↑

infrared (invisible)

red   slightly
           bent
orange

yellow

green

turquoise

blue   strongly
           bent
violet

ultraviolet (invisible)
↓

Breaking up light with a prism, which is a three-sided piece of glass, is possible because of these different waves. As the light passes through the prism, the photons with long wavelengths bend slightly. Those with short wavelengths bend more. If you look at the diagram you can see that this means that the "blue" photons bend the most.

As the photons pass through the prism, they separate and fan out in a band of colour called a colour spectrum.

Make Your Own Prism

We normally think of a prism as a solid triangular wedge of glass or crystal. In fact, anything that's clear and shaped in such a way that it bends and separates light into its different wavelengths (colours) can be a prism. Water can act like a prism, too. That is why you see a rainbow after a rainstorm, in the mist of a waterfall, or in the spray of your garden hose.

Try this on a bright, sunny day. It works best in the morning or late afternoon (when the sun is at an angle).

What You Need

square or rectangular baking pan with a flat bottom
a square or rectangular mirror
water
a small piece of plasticine

What To Do

1. Fill the baking pan with water.

2. Place the pan on the floor in a patch of bright sunlight. Turn the lights in the room off.

3. Lean the mirror against the side of the pan at a steep angle to catch the sun's rays. If the mirror keeps slipping, put a piece of plasticine behind it to hold it in place.

4. Move the mirror around until you see a rainbow appear on the ceiling or wall.

By the way, take a close look at your spectrum. There is no dark purple there. That tells you there are no purple photons. Yet, we do see purple in our everyday life. Your mind creates the colour purple by mixing red and blue photons.

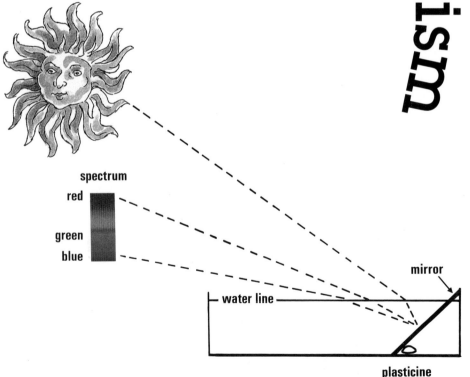

spectrum
red
green
blue

water line

mirror

plasticine

GUESS

What?

The discovery of the spectrum is not new. People have observed the spectrum for thousands of years in natural things such as crystals or rainbows. But Sir Isaac Newton was nearly expelled from the church for daring to suggest what white light was made up of the different colours of the rainbow. In the 1600's people thought that white light was the purest thing on Earth. They believed coloured light was white light that was spoiled.

LET'S DO it!

Create your own white light

What You Need

3 flashlights
3 strong red, green and blue filters
   (either tissue paper, colored
   cellophane or camera filters)
a white wall or a big piece of white
   paper

What to Do

1. Cover each flashlight with a different coloured filter.

2. Make sure your room is dark.

3. Shine the different colours on your wall or paper. Make sure your flashlights are close to the wall and they all overlap.

Primary Colours

White light is made of all the colours of the spectrum but as you saw with the dots on your TV set, it is possible to make white light by mixing just three colours. The TV set uses red, green and blue dots. Many people call these the *primary* colors of light.

When you create different colours of light with your flashlights, or when you watch TV, your cones detect how much of each primary colour is there and they send their signals to your brain. Your brain decides what colour that mixture is.

You have probably been taught that the three *primary* colours are red, blue and *yellow.* Red, blue and yellow are the primary colours of *paint.* If you mix red, blue and yellow paint you will get a dark, murky brown. Try it and see. But when you mix the primary colours of light together, you get white. That is because the rules for mixing coloured lights are very, very different from the rules for mixing coloured paints.

When we mix red and green lights together, we see yellow.

Try it by using two flashlights and red and green filters. Now try mixing red and green paint together. You certainly do not get yellow. In fact, there is no way to get yellow by mixing two colours of paint.

Let's go back to Big Bird on TV and figure out what is going on. You have three types of cones in your retina that contain special chemicals. The

chemicals in your cones become excited by different wavelengths of light. Some are more excited by red light; some are more excited by green light and some are more excited by blue light. Notice that there are no cones for yellow. So why does Big Bird look yellow when we have no yellow cones?

As you saw, on TV he is made up mostly of red and green

yellow light only (coming from real yellow feathers)

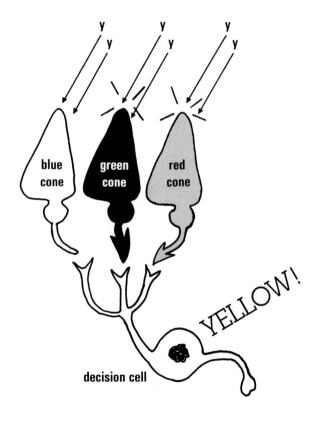

blue cone

green cone

red cone

decision cell

YELLOW!

colour for thousands of years. Big Bird looks yellow because his surface absorbs all the wavelengths of light except the yellow wavelength, and reflects yellow into your eyes.

Look at the spectrum again. Notice that yellow is between red and green. Red cones see red light the best, but they can also see yellow light. Green cones can also see yellow light. The yellow light that enters your eyes excites your red and green cones together—in exactly the same way that the red and green light does from a TV set, and so you see yellow.

dots. If your red and green cones are equally excited by these dots, your brain receives these signals and calls the mixture yellow. That is how we see yellow without having any yellow cones.

Of course, there is another way to see yellow. After all, colour TV has been around for only about 40 years, and human eyes have been seeing

red and green light (coming from 'yellow' feathers on TV)

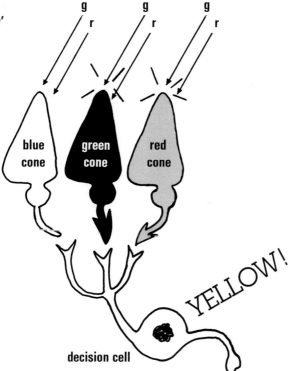

g r g r g r

blue cone green cone red cone

YELLOW!

decision cell

Most people have three types of cones. That was discovered by scientists Young and Helmholtz in the 1800's. Guess what? In 1991, scientists discovered that there are some people who probably have four different types of cones instead of three. Stay tuned for future research!

A Test for Your Red Cones

Some people have trouble seeing certain colours. About eight out of every 100 males and about four out of every 1000 females are born with a colour vision problem that most of us call *colour blindness.* Actually, very few of them are really colour *blind.* They have a problem with one or two or, possibly, all three of their cone types. It is rare for females to be born with colour vision problems.

We are surrounded by people with colour vision problems, yet they are hard to find. That is because, even though they see differently from you, they still use the same colour words. For example, imagine your friend cut his finger, and he is totally red-blind. He will still call the blood red, not because he *sees* red, but because that is the colour we all call blood. For your friend, tomatoes are red for the same reason, but he might also say that an *unripe green* tomato is red!

Try this colour vision test designed to pick up problems in the red cone system. If you are missing red cones you will not be able to see the number 2 hidden in the dots because for your other two cone types all the dots will appear to be the same colour and brightness. Show this to as many boys as you can. There is a good chance one of them cannot see the number. Remember to ask: "what number do you see?", not: "do you see the number 2?"

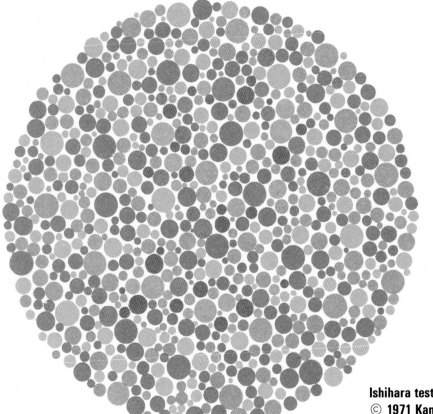

Ishihara test for colour-blindness
© 1971 Kanehara Shuppan Co. Ltd.
Tokyo Japan

GUESS

Making pictures from tiny dots is not new. Take a close look at Georges Seurat's painting, *A Sunday on La Grande Jatte*. He completed it in 1886. This style of painting is called *Pointillism* because every little brush stroke is really a tiny point or dot of colour.

Georges Seurat, *A Sunday on La Grande Jatte*—1884 Helen Birch Bartlett Memorial Collection, 1926, 224 photograph © 1991, The Art Institute of Chicago. All Rights Reserved.

GUESS What?

The colour of your shirt can change depending on the colour surrounding it, and depending on what colour you saw just before.

These two green shirts are exactly the same. But the one surrounded by yellow is a different green than the one surrounded by blue. The colour you see depends on whatever surrounds it.

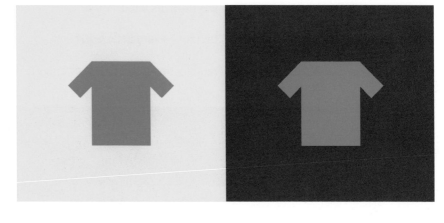

Stare at the black dot in the red shirt and count slowly to 20. Quickly look at the dot on the white shirt. Is it now greenish? Stare at the green shirt for 20 seconds. Does the white shirt now seem reddish or pink? In other words, colour also depends on the colour you saw just before.

LET'S DO it!

This black and white diagram is called Benham's Top. Convince yourself that there is absolutely no colour here—just black and white lines.

What You Need

An exact copy of Benham's Top
a piece of cardboard or Bristol board
a stick sharpened at one end.

What To Do

1. For an exact copy of Benham's Top either make a good photocopy of it, or trace it on a piece of white paper and fill it in as shown.

2. Glue your copy to the cardboard and cut it out.

3. Poke the stick through the exact centre and spin it like a top. It works best in bright sunlight. What's happening to the black lines? Do they suddenly appear to be coloured? Try different speeds to find the strongest colours.

4. Spin it in the opposite direction and watch the lines change colour!

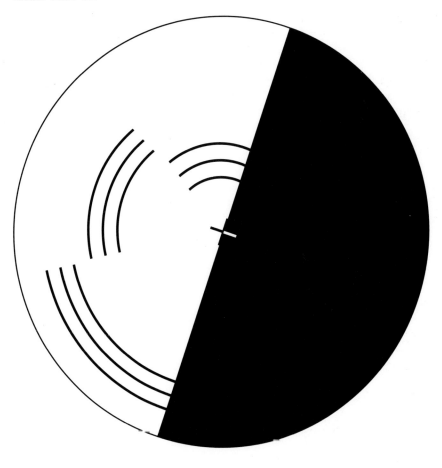

LET'S DO it!

Some colours are easier to see from a distance than others. Convince yourself with this demonstration.

What You Need

sheets of coloured paper: red, yellow, green and blue (Choose colours that are close in brightness.)
paper punch or scissors
glue

Colourful Life Savers

What To Do

1. Use a paper punch to cut out small dots of coloured paper. (If you do not have a paper punch, cut up several small squares, about 1 cm by 1 cm. It is important that they are all *exactly* the same size.)

2. Neatly paste these dots (or squares) onto a piece of white paper. They must not touch and there must be equal space between them. Mix the colours up.

3. Tape the paper at eye level to a wall outside.

4. Slowly walk back from the paper and stop the instant any colour disappears. The blue or yellow pieces will probably disappear first. Continue walking backwards until the reds and greens are no longer colourful. You have just discovered that reds and greens can be much farther away and still be colourful.

What does this have to do with saving a life? If you're stranded in the ocean in a tiny life raft, chances are that if you are spotted, it will be from an airplane way up in the sky in the daytime. What colour life raft would you like to be in? Certainly not blue or yellow. Green would be difficult to spot against the bluish-green of the ocean. Wouldn't a red life raft make the most sense? So why are most life rafts yellow? Sorry, we don't have an answer for that one!

Glossary

adaptation (page 69). The process of getting used to something.

afterimage (page 46). The image that lasts a short time after looking at something bright, or for a long time.

Ames window (page 48). A flat drawing of a window which seems to swing from left to right and back again when it is actually rotating in full circles.

aqueous humour (page 13). The watery liquid between your cornea and lens that feeds the cornea.

Benham's top (page 81). A colourless disc which we see as coloured when spinning.

blind spot (page 23). The place at the optic disk where there are no rods or cones. We are totally blind there.

choroid (page 13). The layer between the retina and sclera which catches unabsorbed light.

cones (page 22). 8 million Nerve cells in the retina which change light into electrical activity. They are mostly in the fovea and 'see' colour.

context (page 43). Information surrounding an object that helps us to understand it.

contrast (page 67). The difference in light between an object and its background.

cornea (page 13). The clear outside bulge in front of the iris. It ats like a lens.

cue (page 51). A clue or hint.

eye muscles (page 13). Three pairs of muscles for each eye which move the eyes about.

focal length (page 15). The distance between any lens and the sharp image of a distant object (anything farther than 6 metres).

fovea (page 23). The central part of the retina we use when we look directly at something. It has the sharpest vision. It sees in colour and only during the day.

glaucoma (page 39). An eye disease which can lead to blindness if untreated. The retina becomes damaged by too much pressure in the eye.

Hermann grid (page 65). A map-like pattern in which 'ghost spots' are seen at the intersections.

iris (page 12). A ring of muscles which opens and closes the pupil. It is the coloured part of the eye.

lens (page 13). The structure just behind the iris which changes its thickness to bring objects at different distances into focus on the retina.

motion aftereffect (page 57). An illusion of motion in which a still object appears to move in one direction after watching something else move in the opposite direction.

motion parallax (page 60). The visual cue to distance which comes from moving through the world.

Necker cube (page 44). A line drawing of a transparent cube which can be seen in two different views.

nerve (page 13). A special cell designed to carry electrical messages through the body.

optic disk (page 13). The place on the retina where the

optic nerve begins. This is the home of the blind spot.

optic nerve (page 13). A thick bundle of one million nerves connecting the retina to the brain.

periphery (page 23). The part of the retina surrounding the fovea designed for seeing at night. It has dull vision but sees motion very well. We are colour blind at its very edges.

perspective (page 49). A cue to depth in which parallel lines appear to meet in the distance.

photons (page 72). The little packages of energy which make up light.

pupil (page 12). The opening in the centre of your iris which lets in light.

retina (page 13). The fine net of nerve cells, including rods and cones, which lines the back of the eye.

rods (page 22). 120 million Nerve cells in the retina which translate light into electrical activity. They are mostly in the periphery and 'see' only black-and-white.

sclera (page 13). The tough, white, outside layer of your eye.

stereo vision (page 34). Seeing depth by combining the slightly different images from each eye.

stereoscope (page 34). Any gadget which shows a different image to the right and left eyes.

vitreous humour (page 13). The crystal clear jelly which fills the eyeball behind the lens.